Real Estate Flipping for Profit

Master the Art of Wealth Creation

Table of Contents

1. Introduction 1

2. The Foundations of Real Estate Flipping 2

   2.1. The Basics of Effective Property Flipping 2

   2.2. Property Acquisition 2

   2.3. Renovation Phase 3

   2.4. Marketing the Property 3

   2.5. Closing the Deal 4

   2.6. Understanding the Real Estate Market 4

   2.7. Risk Management in Real Estate Flipping 4

   2.8. The Laws Around Flipping 5

   2.9. Building a Flipping Team 5

   2.10. Exit Strategies 6

3. Understanding the Real Estate Market 7

   3.1. Understanding Supply and Demand 7

   3.2. Economic Indicators and Real Estate Trends 7

   3.3. Local and Regional Market Dynamics 8

   3.4. Understanding Property Types 8

   3.5. Financing in Real Estate 9

   3.6. Property Evaluation 9

   3.7. Building Your Real Estate Team 9

4. Acquiring Properties: Tips and Tricks 11

   4.1. Understanding Market Dynamics 11

   4.2. Budgeting and Financing Options 12

   4.3. Locating Potential Investment Properties 12

   4.4. Evaluating Potential Investments 13

   4.5. Negotiation and Closing the Deal 13

5. Smart Financing: Managing Money Matters 15

   5.1. Understanding Your Financing Options 15

5.2. Budget Preparation and Cost Management 16

5.3. Analyzing Profitability 16

5.4. Paying your Lenders 17

5.5. Safeguarding Against Risk 17

6. The Art of Property Assessment 18

6.1. Know your Market 18

6.2. Focus on the Locality 18

6.3. Property Inspection 19

6.4. Planning Renovations 19

6.5. Estimating the Costs 19

6.6. Calculating the ARV 20

6.7. The 70% Rule 20

6.8. The Profit Margin 20

6.9. The Intuitive Factor 20

7. Planning a Successful Flip: Renovation Strategies 22

7.1. Understanding the Property's Potential 22

7.2. The Renovation Budget 23

7.3. Prioritizing Renovations 23

7.4. Hiring Professional Help 23

7.5. Staging the Property 24

7.6. Timing the Market 24

7.7. The Importance of Documentation 24

8. Working with Contractors: A Guided Approach 26

8.1. Selecting the Right Contractor 26

8.2. Setting Project Expectations 27

8.3. Contractual Agreements 27

8.4. Navigating Project Execution 28

8.5. Reviewing and Closing the Project 28

9. Staging and Selling: The Final Flip 30

9.1. Understanding Home Staging 30

9.2. Pricing Strategy ... 31

9.3. Creating a Marketing Plan ... 31

9.4. Engaging with Prospective Buyers ... 32

9.5. The Closing Process ... 32

10. Risk Management in Real Estate Flipping ... 34

10.1. Understanding Risk ... 34

10.2. Evaluating Risk ... 34

10.3. Mitigating Risk ... 35

10.4. Implementing Risk Management Tools ... 36

10.5. Continual Risk Assessment ... 36

11. Building your Flipping Empire: Long-Term Strategies ... 37

11.1. Setting up a Robust System ... 37

11.2. Financial Management ... 38

11.3. Building a Skilled Team ... 38

11.4. Balancing Risk with Opportunities ... 38

11.5. Real Estate Market and Location Analysis ... 39

11.6. Continuous Learning ... 39

11.7. Building Relationships ... 39

11.8. Diversification ... 39

Chapter 1. Introduction

In our fascinating Special Report, "Real Estate Flipping for Profit: Master the Art of Wealth Creation," we unravel the mystic threads of property flipping, transforming it from a daunting endeavor into an attainable dream. This isn't an overly technical, hard-to-grasp concept; rather, it's an exciting journey brimming with potential for profit and personal growth. We break down complex strategies into digestible, step-by-step processes that anyone with ambition can follow. With real-life examples, expert advice, and a pinch of cheer, we guide you beyond traditional wealth creation methods towards mastering the art of real estate flipping. Don't miss out on this thrilling expedition towards financial freedom. It's time to turn the key and step into a prosperous future!

Chapter 2. The Foundations of Real Estate Flipping

Flipping real estate is not a casual endeavor. To master this skill, you'll need to dedicate time, resources, and energy to understand the fundamentals, learn from experts, and then execute—and possibly adjust—strategic plans. Let's launch your journey into this fascinating field "brick by rumor-filled brick."

2.1. The Basics of Effective Property Flipping

To begin, let's consider the basic outline of a successful real estate flip. The process often involves four main phases: acquisition, renovation, marketing, and selling. A more in-depth examination of these stages will reveal the intricacies involved in each, enabling you to navigate them more effectively.

2.2. Property Acquisition

Identifying a real estate property worthy of investment is the first step. You're primarily seeking distressed properties, selling at a lower cost because they require renovations.

1. Research: Do not underestimate the power of research; it is the key to discovering great deals. Subscribe to real estate databases and foreclosure lists to get the latest information on potential properties. Cultivate pro-active relationships with real estate auctioneers.

2. Evaluation: Not every distressed property is a hidden gem. You'll need to consider several factors in your evaluation, such as the neighborhood, selected market, potential renovation costs, and

possible profits.

3. Financing: How will you fund your purchase? Options include traditional mortgages, hard money loans, private money loans, and cash investments.

2.3. Renovation Phase

The next step is renovating the acquired property. It can be risky—making it crucial to have a solid renovation plan detailing all identified improvements, the cost, and timeline.

1. Repair: Once a thorough property assessment is done, plan and execute the repairs. Whether it's electrical, plumbing, or structural issues, ensure they are handled professionally.

2. Revamp: A fresh coat of paint can work wonders. So can new fixtures, flooring, and updated appliances. Remember, the goal is to transform this distressed property into something appealing to potential buyers.

3. Professional Help: Attempting to single-handedly carry out renovations could overwhelm you. Hire professionals when necessary. Although it's an additional cost, it may save you in the long run by preventing costly mistakes.

2.4. Marketing the Property

After the renovation, it's time to promote your property. This phase can directly determine your success in flipping the property.

1. Staging: Decorate the property to make it inviting and show off its full potential. A well-presented home can make viewers feel more comfortable and increase its marketability.

2. Pricing: Right pricing is crucial in selling your flipped property. Along with your realtor, research local market prices of homes

similar to yours and set a competitive, reasonable price.

3. Promotion: Make use of various platforms to promote your property. MLS listings, real estate portals, print media, social media, or even hosting an open house are great marketing tactics.

2.5. Closing the Deal

Now it's time to sell. Negotiating and signing the deal is a tense, often complex phase, but, with the right approach, you can turn it into a success.

1. Negotiation: Don't be offended by low offers or critique. Instead, calmly negotiate and offer solid reasons for your counter-offers.

2. Legalities: Engage a lawyer who specializes in property sales to help you navigate the legal procedures.

3. Patience: Understand that closing a property deal can take time. Patience is crucial.

2.6. Understanding the Real Estate Market

The real estate market is subject to numerous factors, including economic trends, interest rates, and even local preferences. Grasping these complexities will help you anticipate trends and time your flips for optimal profitability.

2.7. Risk Management in Real Estate Flipping

To successfully flip real estate, you must learn to anticipate and manage risks. These can include unexpected renovation costs, a longer-than-expected time to sell the property, or a sudden dip in the real estate market.

1. Diversify: Avoid putting all your eggs in one basket. Having more than one property in diverse geographical locations can help mitigate losses if one market undergoes a downturn.

2. Stay Informed: Regularly updating yourself with market news can help forecast market trends, thus mitigating risks.

3. Emergency Fund: Always have an emergency fund to cover unexpected expenses. This fund minimizes financial stress and provides a safety net.

2.8. The Laws Around Flipping

It is important to understand the legal implications of flipping real estate. Familiarize yourself with local and national laws to avoid penalties or legal complications.

1. Understand tax implications: Flipping properties is considered a business operation and therefore subject to applicable state and federal taxes.

2. Permits and legal requirements: Ensuring all renovations meet local codes and standards is crucial.

3. Ethical considerations: Honest transactions build your reputation in the industry.

2.9. Building a Flipping Team

Building a profitable enterprise requires collaboration. Surround yourself with a well-rounded team: real estate agents, contractors, real estate attorneys, accountants, and potential investors.

2.10. Exit Strategies

An exit strategy is a contingency plan, defined in case a property investment does not proceed as planned. This could be renting or leasing, seller financing, or wholesaling the property.

Flipping properties may appear daunting initially, but armed with the right knowledge, technical and practical understanding, a solid strategy, and a reliable team, you are well on your way to mastering this wealth-creation art. Embrace the journey, grow from the challenges, and savor the thrill of closing the deal. Welcome to the world of Real Estate Flipping!

Chapter 3. Understanding the Real Estate Market

Before diving into the money-making business of real estate flipping, it's crucial to have an in-depth understanding of the real estate market. This chapter synthesizes a wealth of information to create a comprehensive guide that equips you with the understanding needed to successfully navigate the challenging arena of property investments.

3.1. Understanding Supply and Demand

The real estate market, like any other market, operates on the principles of supply and demand. Real estate supply comprises the number of properties available for purchase, and demand the number of willing and able buyers. These two variables are constantly fluctuating due to a complex interplay of socio-economic factors.

High demand coupled with low supply results in increased property prices and a seller's market. On the flip side, high supply and low demand lower prices, creating a buyer's market. It's crucial for real estate flippers to accurately gauge the state of the market, enabling favorable buying and selling choices.

3.2. Economic Indicators and Real Estate Trends

To navigate the real estate market successfully, you need to interpret various economic indicators that provide insight into the overall economy's health. General economic conditions, unemployment rates, interest rates, inflation, and consumer confidence all significantly impact property pricing.

For instance, low-interest rates make borrowing for property investments cheaper, often leading to a surge in demand and, subsequently, increased property prices. Conversely, high unemployment rates can decrease demand as fewer people can afford to buy houses, hence dampening property prices.

It's also important to stay up-to-date with real estate trends that influence property demand. These trends include technological advancements, changing work or lifestyle habits, demographic shifts, and urban development plans.

3.3. Local and Regional Market Dynamics

Apart from understanding national economic indicators and trends, it's crucial to familiarize yourself with local and regional market dynamics. Variables such as neighborhood attractiveness, school district quality, crime rates, and proximity to amenities can impact house prices significantly.

Real estate is often very localized, and prices can vary greatly even within the same city. Researching the local housing market, including current and future infrastructural developments, can provide valuable insights that inform your flipping strategy.

3.4. Understanding Property Types

Different property types present unique opportunities and challenges for flippers. Residential properties, such as single-family houses, duplexes, triplexes, and townhouses, are popular among flippers due to their broad demand base. Commercial and industrial properties, on the other hand, require higher investments upfront but can offer considerable returns.

Understanding your target market's property type preferences can significantly enhance the success of your flipping venture.

3.5. Financing in Real Estate

Solid understanding of financing options is vital in the flipping business. Traditional mortgage options, hard money lenders, private money lenders, and real estate crowdfunding are some of the financing routes that an investor can explore.

Understanding the interest rates, loan-to-value (LTV) ratios, points, and loan origination fees associated with these various financing options can help you choose the best financing pathway.

3.6. Property Evaluation

The intrinsic value of a house isn't always reflected in its price. A property evaluation will help you identify underpriced properties ripe for flipping. Look for properties you can add value to through renovations and upgrades.

Property evaluation entails assessing the property's physical condition, its location, estimated repair costs, the market value after renovations (After Repair Value, or ARV), and your potential profit.

3.7. Building Your Real Estate Team

No individual can single-handedly handle all the aspects of real estate flipping. A real estate team typically consists of a real estate agent, mortgage broker, property inspector, contractor, and attorney. Establishing a team plays a crucial role in making informed decisions throughout the flipping process.

Understanding the real estate market is more than grasping its technical aspects — it involves understanding wider social, economic, and local factors that impact property prices. With this knowledge, you'll gain an edge in your real estate flipping venture, pinpointing lucrative opportunities and devising strategies to maximize your profits effectively.

Chapter 4. Acquiring Properties: Tips and Tricks

Before diving into the crux of property acquisition, it's crucial to acknowledge that real estate flipping is an entrepreneurial venture. As such, it demands a fair share of business acumen, dedication, and foresight. This chapter is intended as a comprehensive guide on property acquisition, offering a plethora of how-to's, tips, and tricks. We start with the basics: understanding the marketplace, recognizing trends, and setting your financial compass in the right direction.

4.1. Understanding Market Dynamics

Property markets are affected by a variety of dynamics, including economic cycles, demographic trends, interest rates, and government policies. As a real estate investor, you need to keep your finger on the pulse of these market dynamics.

1. Economic Cycles: Be aware of the general state of the economy. A strong economy often implies low unemployment and high wages, which leads to higher demand for properties.

2. Demographic Trends: Keep an eye on changes in the local population, age distribution, income levels, and family size. These demographics will determine the kind of properties in demand.

3. Interest Rates: Lower interest rates often stimulate housing market activity because they reduce the cost of mortgage financing.

4. Government Policies: Policies on taxes, subsidies, and zoning can significantly impact property values. Stay informed about these, too.

Take time to regularly research and stay updated on these factors.

4.2. Budgeting and Financing Options

With a solid understanding of market dynamics, the next step is setting up a budget and investigating financing options. Start by evaluating your financial standing and determining the maximum amount you can manage for an investment. Prepare a realistic budget that includes not only the property's purchase price but also renovation expenses, holding costs, and potential unforeseen expenses.

Next, identify financing avenues. Conventional mortgages, home equity loans, or hard money loans from private lenders are all viable options. Each has its pros and cons; evaluate these in light of your financial situation and investment goals.

4.3. Locating Potential Investment Properties

Finding a property with good return potential is perhaps the most challenging part. Unlike regular home buying, you're not looking for a ready-to-move-in home. Instead, you're looking for a home that needs work but resides in a good location.

1. Leverage online property listing portals: Websites like Zillow and Realtor.com provide information on property specifications, neighborhood details, and historic selling prices.

2. Enlist the help of a real estate agent: Real estate agents have access to Multiple Listing Service (MLS), a database which publishes property listing information before it reaches the general public.

3. Drive or walk around target neighborhoods: Driving for dollars is a time-honored technique. It's an uncomplicated, though time-consuming, way of finding off-market properties.

4.4. Evaluating Potential Investments

After locating potential properties, the next step is a thorough evaluation. This phase requires you to delve deeper into aspects of the property that could impact your profit margins.

1. Assess the Location: Location is paramount. Consider factors like proximity to amenities, schools, and business centers, crime rates, and future local development plans.

2. Estimate Repair Costs: Always get a professional inspection. They help in the assessment of the property's condition and estimate repair costs.

3. Identify the After Repair Value (ARV): This is what the property might sell for after restoration. There are online tools, and local real estate agents can provide accurate ARVs.

4. Calculate Potential Profit: Subtract your expected costs (purchase, renovation, holding) from the ARV. If the numbers add up to a significant profit, consider proceeding with the purchase.

4.5. Negotiation and Closing the Deal

The final step in the acquisition process is negotiation and closing the deal. This phase involves making an offer, negotiating with the seller or their agent, and finalizing the sale contract. Remember to maintain a business-like approach during the negotiation process. Understand the seller's motivations and leverage that knowledge to swing the deal in your favor. Also, involving a real estate lawyer can prevent potential legal issues later.

In closing, acquiring properties for flipping is an exciting endeavor. It involves market research, financial planning, painstaking scouting, thorough evaluation, and skillful negotiation. Each aspect is essential in paving the way for successful real estate flipping. This chapter equips you with the tips and tricks you need to navigate this journey, from the first step to your final destination — a profitable flip. Remember, practice and patience are your best friends in this venture.

Chapter 5. Smart Financing: Managing Money Matters

The first secret of successful real estate flipping lies neatly concealed in the understanding of financing. It's not just about buying low and selling high, but about how you manage your monetary matters thoughtfully. Think of investing as a journey, and your financing avenues as your vehicle - to travel the path swiftly and safely, you must know your vehicle first.

5.1. Understanding Your Financing Options

Before stepping into the world of property flipping, explore all the financing options available to you and understand the cost and profitability associated with them. Here is a list of common real estate financing choices:

- Hard Money Loans: These types of loans are commonly used in real estate flipping because they can be received quickly and used to purchase properties that may not qualify for traditional financing. However, they often come with higher interest rates, meaning the cost of the loan needs to be carefully considered.

- Private Money Loans: These loans typically come from people you know, such as friends, family, or personal connections. Private money loans often offer flexible terms and lower interests rates compared to hard money loans, but they can complicate personal relationships if your real estate flip doesn't go as planned.

- Traditional Bank Loans: If you can qualify for a traditional bank loan, this can often be the cheapest financing option. However, these loans can be harder to secure, require a longer approval process, and may not cover the cost of repairs needed for a property flip.

- Cash: If you have enough savings, this is the most straightforward financing method. It eliminates the need to pay interest, but it also exposes you to a greater financial risk.

5.2. Budget Preparation and Cost Management

Knowing the amount you can afford is important, but equally crucial is understanding the expenses associated with a flip and figuring out a budget. A successful real estate flip incorporates a comprehensive budget that covers

- Purchase price

- Cost of necessary repairs

- Holding costs

- Marketing costs

- Closing costs

Be prepared. Don't get caught off guard with unanticipated repairs because surprises can often emerge during renovations.

5.3. Analyzing Profitability

Develop techniques to rapidly estimate the potential profitability of a property. This involves calculating the After Repair Value (ARV), estimate of repairs (EOR), and the Maximum Allowable Offer (MAO).

- ARV is the projected value of the property after all repairs have been made.

- EOR includes all repair and remodeling costs.

- MAO is the maximum amount you can pay for the property and still make a profit, calculated by subtracting repair costs, holding and closing costs, and desired profit from the ARV.

Establish strict criteria and constantly revise them as you gain more experience in the industry and market conditions change.

5.4. Paying your Lenders

Devise a concrete plan for your exit strategy, i.e., selling the property before even purchasing it. The profits serve two main purposes - paying back the lenders and providing you the profit from the flip. Repaying your lenders promptly and fully fosters a solid relationship based on trust. Always remember, a good reputation in the real estate business is invaluable.

5.5. Safeguarding Against Risk

Any investment comes with risks, and real estate is no exception. Incorporate risk mitigation strategies in your business model. This can include diversifying your property investments, purchasing insurance, account for extra time and budget for unexpected complications, and never over-leveraging yourself financially.

Understanding, strategizing and managing finances is pivotal in your quest to prevail in the real estate flipping industry. Remember, every successful investor was once a novice and through planning, cautious decision-making, and driven by their ambition, they were able to master the financial aspect of flipping. You can do it too!

Chapter 6. The Art of Property Assessment

Thoroughly assessing any property you're considering for a flipping project is crucial. Miscalculations or avoiding proper due diligence can cost you dearly. We emphasize both qualitative and quantitative aspects; it's not only about the maths, but also understanding the area, the property, and its potential that will get you closer to profitable real estate flipping.

6.1. Know your Market

Understanding the real estate market is the first step before you dive into property assessment. This involves a broad view of overall real estate trends, and further drilling into the specific area or neighborhood where your potential flip property is located. Researching current property prices, how long houses are staying on the market, which properties are selling quickly, and the kind of homes buyers are looking for, will give you a good sense of the market pulse. In particular, focus on patterns and trends that might impact your investment—recent developments, zoning laws, and changes in the local economy.

6.2. Focus on the Locality

Possible buyers will consider more than just the house; they'll look at the entire package—the locality. Elements that increase the selling potential include proximity to amenities such as schools, parks, shopping districts, hospitals and public transportation. Areas with a thriving community or a low crime rate hold greater appeal. Understanding the neighborhood, its residents, their lifestyle, and needs help in tailoring your flip property to resonate better with potential buyers.

6.3. Property Inspection

A detailed property inspection is a non-negotiable component of the assessment process. Hire a certified property inspector who can help identify current and potential issues. These could range from foundational problems to roofing, plumbing or wiring issues. The inspection report will help you estimate costs for repair and renovation. Make sure to attend the inspection to learn about the property first hand.

6.4. Planning Renovations

Once you have the inspection report in hand, it's time to plan the renovation. Prioritize repairs that increase the value of the home. Kitchens and bathrooms, for instance, pack a sizeable return on investment. It's not just about making everything new, but making smart choices that enhance the property's value without blowing your budget. If you're not scared of a little DIY work, you can save significantly, but be realistic about what you can handle, and hire professionals where necessary.

6.5. Estimating the Costs

Next, calculate your costs. First, consider your purchase price and financing costs. Add renovation costs, which should include materials, labor, permits, and contingency for unforeseen issues. Don't forget costs like property taxes, utilities, insurance, staging and selling costs, and any potential carrying costs if the property doesn't sell immediately.

By being diligent about the cost estimation process, you can avoid unwanted surprises halfway through the flipping process.

6.6. Calculating the ARV

The After Repair Value (ARV) is the price you expect to sell the property for after renovations. This is a critical variable in determining whether a project is worth the investment. Research recent sales of similar, renovated properties in the area to get a realistic ARV.

6.7. The 70% Rule

One popular guideline among house flippers is the 70% rule. This suggests that a flipper should pay no more than 70% of the ARV, minus the cost of repairs. While not an absolute, it can be a useful guide in making quick estimates.

6.8. The Profit Margin

Finally, calculate your potential profit. Subtract your total costs from the ARV. It's not enough for this number to be positive; it should be significantly enough so that it compensates for the risk, time, and effort you've put into acquiring, renovating, and selling the property.

Ideally, aim for a profit of at least 20% of the ARV. If the numbers don't add up, it might be best to walk away and wait for a better opportunity.

6.9. The Intuitive Factor

Numbers indeed play a crucial role, but successful flipping also demands intuition trained by experience. An experienced flipper can sense potential in a house that others may overlook. As you flip more properties, you'll develop this intuitive understanding, which when combined with solid assessment strategies, can lead to impressive profits.

Always remember, property assessment isn't merely about ticking off a checklist; it's about diving deep into the process, understanding the potential and the roadblocks, and having a clear plan. It's an art, and mastering it can pave your way to a prosperous future in real estate flipping.

Chapter 7. Planning a Successful Flip: Renovation Strategies

Taking the leap into the realm of property flipping is a venture composed of various elements. Among these elements, planning a successful flip and identifying effective renovation strategies form the core of one's flipping endeavors. This comprehensive guide aims to light the path leading to that lucrative income you've been fantasizing about.

7.1. Understanding the Property's Potential

Before bringing out the toolbox and calling in the painters, it's imperative to assess the property's potential. The secret to successful property flipping lies in maximizing returns by enhancing the property without overspending on non-essential features. To ace this, consider the following:

1. Neighborhood: How does the property compare to others in the same area? You need to see the overall picture rather than focusing on individual elements. After all, there's no point in having the best house on a run-down block.

2. Local Market Conditions: Know your market well. Are property prices rising or declining? The current market scenario significantly affects the success of your flip.

3. Property Age and Condition: Run a thorough property inspection with trusted experts. Old isn't always gold, especially when it comes to real estate.

7.2. The Renovation Budget

Allocating budget judiciously is an art. Stick to the 70% rule in house flipping, i.e., the Maximum Purchase Price = 70% of the After Repair Value (ARV) - Repair Costs.

Keep the budget tight but be realistic. Every property will throw up unexpected costs, ranging from essential repairs to local fees. It's wise to factor in a contingency fund of at least 10-20% of the project's total anticipated cost to cover such expenses.

7.3. Prioritizing Renovations

To make a property splash in the market, certain features demand more attention — and budgeting — than others. Know what's worth investing in:

1. Kitchens and Bathrooms: These are deal-makers or breakers in property flipping. A modern, functional kitchen and clean, appealing bathrooms significantly increase a property's value.

2. Flooring: Worn out or outdated flooring is an immediate deterrent. Invest in good quality, lasting flooring materials that resonate with buyers' tastes.

3. Structural Repairs: Structural issues can be a bottomless pit, turning your potentially profitable flip into a costly nightmare. Assess these costs at the outset and plan accordingly.

7.4. Hiring Professional Help

While DIY might seem cost-effective at first, it may lead to more expenses down the line if not done properly. Unless you're an expert, hire professionals for plumbing, electrical, and structural work. Not only does this ensure quality, it also adheres to safety regulations and standards essential for property selling.

7.5. Staging the Property

Staging a property involves strategically arranging furniture and decor to highlight its best features. While optional, a well-staged property accelerates the selling process and can fetch higher bids.

1. Furniture: Avoid over-stuffing rooms; create spaciousness. Use functional, contemporary furniture to impart a fresh, appealing look.

2. Decor: Keep the decor minimalistic and in tune with the latest trends.

3. Lighting: Make use of natural light as much as possible. Where needed, use soft, warm lights for a cozy ambience.

7.6. Timing the Market

The best time to sell a flipped property varies by location. Study local market trends and find the sweet spot. For instance, warmer months may be the peak selling season in areas experiencing harsh winters. Align your renovation to coincide with these periods.

7.7. The Importance of Documentation

Keep track of all expenses, no matter how trivial they may seem. The flipping game demands that you account for every penny. Additionally, robust documentation serves as a shield from tax audit troubles.

Getting your feet wet in the property flipping venture demands grit, strategy, and vision. Smart renovations are the bridge that connects a rundown property with its glorious potential. As with any journey, there will unexpected turns and challenges. But with this comprehensive guide on renovation strategies, overcoming these bumps will prove not only feasible, but also immensely rewarding.

25

Chapter 8. Working with Contractors: A Guided Approach

Before diving into the intricacies of working with contractors, it's crucial to understand the importance these professionals play in the flipping process. Acquiring and selling properties is only a portion of the real estate flipping equation. The integral part lies in enhancing the value of the property, which necessitates substantial renovation work. This is where contractors come into the picture, applying their skills to turn your property into a desirable and profitable venture. So, let's break this big concept down, detailing each facet of working with contractors and its significance.

8.1. Selecting the Right Contractor

Finding the right contractor is like choosing a business partner: you must carefully assess their credentials, past work, and overall fit with your project. Remember, a contractor can make or break your property's transformation.

When beginning your contractor search, word-of-mouth referrals provide the most promising leads. Reach out to network connections, colleagues, and friends in the industry. Local real estate investors or agents are also terrific sources of trusted contractor recommendations.

Doing a thorough background check is equally important. Consider this as a mini-audit—verify licenses, check for pending lawsuits, go over online reviews and ratings, or even connect with their previous clients. Additionally, check their financial stability to ensure they won't bail halfway through your project due to financial problems.

8.2. Setting Project Expectations

Defining clear project plans and expectations is an essential step within contractor engagement. Draw up a detailed work plan with defined deadlines, budgets, and project needs. This plan will act as a blueprint for the construction phase, encompassing the contractor's obligations as well as your project's specific nuances.

Timelines are paramount, but you should also involve the contractor in setting realistic deadlines, considering both their capabilities and your urgency to flip the property. Imposing unfeasible deadlines might lead to rushed, substandard work.

Budgeting is another aspect where mutual agreement is indispensable. During the negotiation process, resist the temptation to choose the cheapest offer-- remember that in construction, you often get what you pay for.

8.3. Contractual Agreements

When you've settled on a contractor that matches your project's requirements, it's time to make it official via a comprehensive, legally binding agreement. The contract is not only commercial insurance but also a documentation of expectations and terms. Both parties must thoroughly review the contract to ensure all project specifics are accurately represented.

Key elements of the contract should include detailed specifics of the job, a schedule of payments, project deadlines, contingencies for unexpected concerns, and liability in case of accidents on site, among other details.

Ensure that any changes or variations from the initial plan throughout the project are tracked and approved through Change Orders. This keeps the original contract as the master document, thus avoiding misunderstandings and disputes.

8.4. Navigating Project Execution

The construction phase is where the partnership with the contractor truly materializes. Ensure constant communication throughout the project execution. Regular site visits and periodical meetings help maintain project alignment. Use these opportunities to review progress, address concerns, and realign expectations.

It's also crucial to understand that construction projects rarely execute perfectly according to plan. There may be setbacks, unexpected structural issues, or cost overruns. In such cases, having a contingency fund and maintaining calm is essential.

8.5. Reviewing and Closing the Project

Upon project completion, conduct a meticulous walkthrough with your contractor, noting any discrepancies or uncompleted tasks. Make sure everything is finished to your satisfaction before making the final payment. Don't overlook little details; these are what prospective buyers will notice.

Thereafter, ensure all closing formalities are undertaken - warranty documentation, post-completion cleanup, and confirmation that all subcontractors have been paid (to avoid future lien claims on your property).

Working with contractors is a challenging yet rewarding aspect of property flipping. By choosing the right contractor, setting clear expectations, and keeping the lines of communication open, you can avoid potential pitfalls and ensure your project stays on track towards success.

Remember, every successful flip brings you one step closer to mastering the art of this wealth creation avenue. So, as you step into your next project, keep these guidelines in hand, regardless of whether you're a seasoned flipper or a novice in the field. With the right knowledge, tools, and people by your side, even the most formidable property challenge can be flipped into a profitable venture.

Chapter 9. Staging and Selling: The Final Flip

Let's begin by focusing on the heart of the operation: understanding the importance of staging and selling in the realm of flipping properties. This encapsulates everything from preparing the property for visualization by prospective buyers, to employing effective marketing strategies, to completing the sales transaction. While this might seem daunting, as with any other phase of property flipping, it can be simplified with effective planning, the right strategies, and execution.

9.1. Understanding Home Staging

Home staging is an integral part of the sales process. This strategy entails presenting the home in an attractive, welcoming manner. It allows potential buyers to envision themselves and their belongings in the space, thereby eliciting strong emotions that could influence their buying decision.

An effectively staged home differentiates itself from unoccupied, bare, or poorly furnished houses. The visual appeal and the feeling of comfort and homeliness this exercise delivers may potentially verify the asking price to the buyer, expedite the sales process, or even spark a bidding war.

You do not necessarily need an interior designer to create a captivating look. However, understanding the basics of home staging and working within a budget can go a long way.

1. Declutter: Always begin by decluttering the property. Remove personal items and any unnecessary furniture to create a spacious feel.

2. Neutral Palette: Opt for a neutral color scheme to appeal to a

broader audience. This allows potential buyers to imagine how they would personalize the space.

3. Highlight Key Features: If the property has unique features like a fireplace or built-in shelves, ensure these are not lost in the staging process. Rather, highlight them.

4. Outdoor Appeal: Do not forget the exterior. A neat garden or a welcoming porch can set the right first impression.

9.2. Pricing Strategy

Pricing a flipped property can be a tricky process. Set the price too high, and it could deter buyers; too low, and you risk losing potential profit. It is crucial to understand the local real estate market, recent sales in the area, and the value added through the renovation.

1. Comparative Market Analysis (CMA): CMA allows you to compare your property against others recently sold in the area with similar features and dimensions.

2. Professional Appraisal: Hiring a professional appraiser can give you a defensible pricing estimate based on the current state of the property post-renovation.

9.3. Creating a Marketing Plan

Once the home is staged and priced, the next step centers around attracting potential buyers through a well-thought-out marketing plan.

1. High-Quality Visuals: Employ professional photographers to capture the essence of your flipped property. Well-shot, vibrant photos can substantially enhance your online and offline listings.

2. Virtual Tours: With the advent of technology and in the wake of recent social changes, offer virtual tours of the property. This will

allow prospective buyers to view the property without physically being present.

3. Social Media Visibility: In our digitally interconnected era, do not forget about the power of social media. Platforms such as Facebook and Instagram can help spread the word about your property.

4. Multiple Listing Service (MLS): The MLS is a tool that allows real estates brokers to share information about properties they are selling. This exposure to a broad network can significantly enhance your sales opportunities.

9.4. Engaging with Prospective Buyers

Engaging with potential buyers is a delicate art. It requires a balance of patience, negotiation skills, transparency, and salesmanship.

1. Open House: Consider hosting open houses and private viewings. This offers potential buyers an unpressured environment to explore the property.

2. Transparency: Be forthright about the renovations carried out, the use of materials, and the condition of appliances. Transparency facilitates trust and can lead to a smoother sales process.

9.5. The Closing Process

The final step in selling your flip property marks the closing process. This involves satisfactory home inspection reports, acquiring necessary approvals, meeting legal obligations, and signing stacks of paperwork.

1. Home Inspection: Most buyers will require a home inspection

before finalizing the sale. The home inspector takes an in-depth look at the house, checking for defects or issues.

2. Closing Costs: The closing costs typically range from 2% to 5% of the loan amount. These costs include fees for handling the paperwork, title search, and insurance coverage.

3. Transfer of Ownership: This involves signing the deed over to the new homeowner from the seller, thus marking the final part of the property flipping journey.

Remember, flipping real estate is not just about making profit but also about adding value to properties, creating dream homes for others, and contributing to the vitality of the community. It is this balance of ambition and altruism that makes the process genuinely gratifying. Following strategic staging and selling steps, harnessing market understanding, and maintaining a positive attitude will enable you to master the art of wealth creation through flipping homes.

Chapter 10. Risk Management in Real Estate Flipping

In any investment venture, managing risk effectively is crucial, and real estate flipping is no exception. Acknowledging the uncertainties and devising strategies to combat them will streamline your journey to success.

10.1. Understanding Risk

The first step in managing risk is understanding what it entails. Risk, in simple terms, pertains to the potential for something to go wrong. In real estate flipping, this could mean a multitude of things, including unanticipated renovation costs, fluctuation in the property market, contractor issues, and changes in government laws and regulations.

Perhaps the property you thought was a great deal turns out to need expensive foundation repairs, or maybe the neighborhood's property value suddenly plunges. In other instances, the contractor might default, or an unexpected zoning regulation could prevent you from making desired modifications. These potential adverse events can drastically affect your profits or even result in losses.

10.2. Evaluating Risk

Once you understand what risks might be in play, the next step involves evaluation. A thorough risk assessment should be conducted for every property before acquisition. The following are some of the key areas you should focus on:

1. Property condition: Consider conducting a professional home inspection to identify potential issues with the property that

could lead to additional costs in renovation.

2. Market research: Understand the demand-supply dynamics in local and national real estate markets. Analyze recent sales and price trends in the area to avoid investing in locations with declining property values.

3. Zoning and legal issues: Seek guidance from a real estate attorney or an expert to navigate through any regulatory or legal complexities concerning the property.

4. Financial analysis: Do not just calculate the potential profit but also consider the costs involved. These might include inspection fees, renovation costs, marketing expenses, legal fees, and the time value of money.

10.3. Mitigating Risk

After identifying and evaluating the risks, the next phase involves planning for risk mitigation. Here's how you can alleviate some of the prevalent risks in property flipping:

1. Budget Planning: Conservative budget planning can save you from many unanticipated expenses. Always allow margin for cost overruns and unexpected expenses.

2. Choosing Professionals: Whether a real estate agent, contractor, or attorney, ensure you are partnering with licensed, insured, experienced professionals with a solid reputation in the industry.

3. Diversification: Don't put all your eggs in one basket. It makes sense to diversify your investments across varied real estate market segments and geographies.

4. Exit Strategy: Every business plan must include an exit strategy, and flipping real estate is no different. You should have strategies lined up for both positive and negative scenarios.

10.4. Implementing Risk Management Tools

It's one thing to outline your risk management strategy and another to enforce it consistently. There are tools and techniques designed to aid in risk management that you should consider.

One effective tool is insurance. Before starting any renovation work, ensure your property and project are adequately insured. This will provide you protection against unexpected adversities.

Another strategy includes setting up a Limited Liability Company (LLC) for your flipping business. The LLC helps protect your personal assets from being targeted in the event of a lawsuit or financial hardship related to business operations.

10.5. Continual Risk Assessment

Risk in real estate flipping is an ongoing process, not a one-time event. As the market evolves and project issues arise, continually assessing and adjusting your risk management strategy is essential.

Regularly revisiting and updating your approach supports progressive improvements in your real estate business's risk culture. Continual risk assessment helps in making informed decisions and strengthens your preparation for potential adverse circumstances.

In summary, effective risk management is a crucial component in the real estate flipping venture. By understanding, evaluating, mitigating, and continually assessing risk, you can turn potential pitfalls into opportunities while inspiring confidence and encouraging growth. Remember, it's not just about avoiding risk but knowing how to navigate it productively.

Chapter 11. Building your Flipping Empire: Long-Term Strategies

In your early days of property flipping, the primary focus often lays in understanding the basics, getting your hands dirty with a few first deals. However, to build a real estate empire, you need to develop and execute long-term strategies. Let's dive into the major realms to consider as you create a sustainable property flipping business and evolve it into a thriving empire.

11.1. Setting up a Robust System

Effective flipping isn't about one-off victorious deals - it's about creating a system that consistently identifies appealing properties, accurately assesses repair costs, effectively renovates, and rapidly resells for profit. This process, like any system, consists of several components that must work together seamlessly.

1. Finding Profitable Properties: You'll need to master using various sources such as Multiple Listing Services (MLS), foreclosures, auctions, and wholesalers to discover promising properties.

2. Estimating Repairs: With time and experience, you'll get better at predicting repair costs. One smart approach is partnering with reliable contractors who can offer accurate estimates.

3. Financing: You need to stay aware of various financing options like hard money lenders, private lenders, or traditional banks to fund your deals effectively.

4. Renovation: Having a trustworthy and competent crew would be beneficial. This includes contractors, real estate agents, lawyers, and accountants, among others.

5. Resale: A competent real estate agent can alleviate the pressure of resale. Choosing an agent with a good track record in your property's neighborhood can be invaluable.

11.2. Financial Management

Real estate flipping is a business and should be treated as such when it comes to financial management. Maintain separate accounts for your real estate activity and always keep a strict tab on your cash inflows and outflows. Accurate bookkeeping is non-negotiable for sustained success in this industry. Considering hiring a good accountant can save you a lot of trouble down the line, as can investing in property management software to keep track of your expenses.

11.3. Building a Skilled Team

As you grow, you can't do everything alone. You will need a team. The size of your team largely depends on your goals and resources. Initially, your team may include a real estate agent, a home inspector, and a trustworthy contractor. As you expand, you might consider adding a real estate attorney, an accountant, and perhaps workers for your rehab projects. Your team will be instrumental in your journey, so choose wisely.

11.4. Balancing Risk with Opportunities

Risk management is crucial in real estate flipping. While every deal carries a risk, successful investors know how to balance risk with potential rewards. Can the property be resold quickly? Can it yield desirable profits after all the rehab costs? Learn to assess potential risks, including market conditions, before moving forward.

11.5. Real Estate Market and Location Analysis

Understanding the real estate market and the influence location plays is vital. Analyzing factors like employment rates, neighborhood development plans, schools, crime rates, property taxes, or local amenities can help in making informed decisions.

11.6. Continuous Learning

The real estate industry is dynamic, with the market, regulations, and trends constantly changing. By staying informed and continuously learning, you can better adapt and make decisions that drive your business forward. Attend workshops and seminars, read industry reports and follow influential real estate blogs to gain real-time insights.

11.7. Building Relationships

Network with other real estate investors, join local real estate groups, attend meetings, and participate in online forums. Building relationships can provide you with invaluable advice, partnership opportunities, and a support system.

11.8. Diversification

To mitigate risk and broaden your earning potential, consider diversifying your portfolio. This could include venturing into different types of properties, such as commercial properties, rental properties, or different locations.

It is important to remember that building an empire doesn't happen overnight. It requires dedication, patience, and the ability to adapt and grow. Stay committed to learning and refining your strategies, and with time, you can create an impressive real estate flipping empire.

www.ingramcontent.com/pod-product-compliance
Lightning Source LLC
Chambersburg PA
CBHW071032260726
48661CB00007B/3006